howTo be a friend

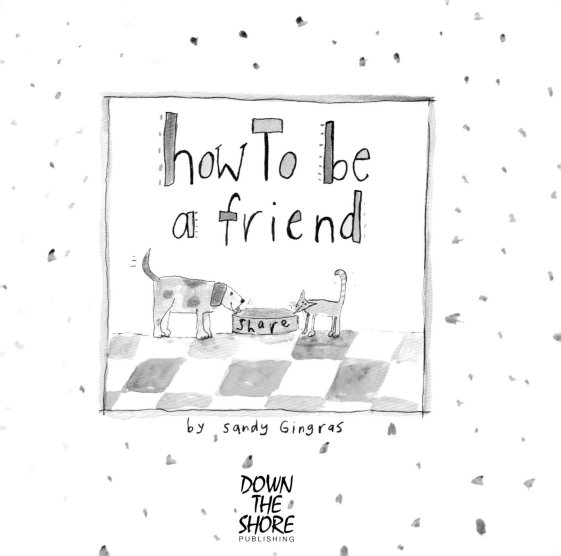

Down The Shore Publishing Corp.
Box 3100, Harvey Cedars, NJ 08008
www.down-the-shore.com

The words "Down The Shore" and the Down The Shore Publishing logo
are a registered U.S. Trademark.

Printed in China
2 4 6 8 10 9 7 5 3 1
First Printing

Library of Congress Cataloging-in-Publication Data

Gingras, Sandy, 1958-
How to be a friend / by Sandy Gingras.
p. cm.
ISBN 0-945582-99-4
1. Friendship. I. Title.
BF575.F66G56 2003
177'.62--dc21
2003048476

To doLLy and biLLy

for Their Love and LighT

My first friend was invisible. She lived in our kitchen pantry between the cereal boxes. She was bratty and free in every way that I wanted to be. I brought her my best stories and favorite marbles, and she turned everything on the shelves upside down and got me into trouble.

From her, I learned that

a friend changes you invisibly.
She got me to whisper secrets
from way down in my hearT, showed
me how To Laugh about nothing,
how to Listen To what wasn't said.
She taught me how The best
things in Life are simple and
righT nexT To us and are offen
the hardest to see.

To risk The chancy
Times of Sun
and rain

and become buds.

To commit to some common ground but

To blossom into difference

Friendship is a going ahead with no map on a journey full of Twisty Turns, Loop-de-Loops, dead ends and detours.

Allow for ups and downs.

wheee

Have some play in your steering wheel

Savor Sweet Silences

Bask in The Sunny SpoTs

They make iT aLL worThwhiLe.

forgive

with grace

Learn how To bounce

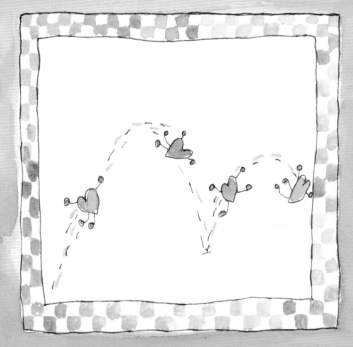

and To remember when...

Know when a LiTTLe nudge

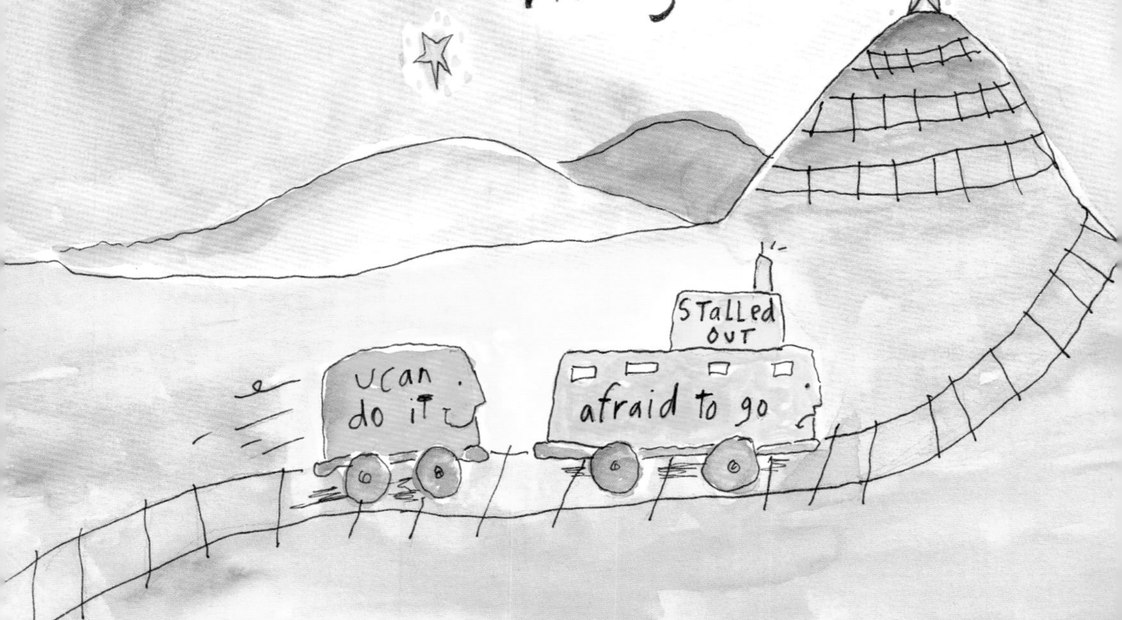

can be a big heLp

Light a way home

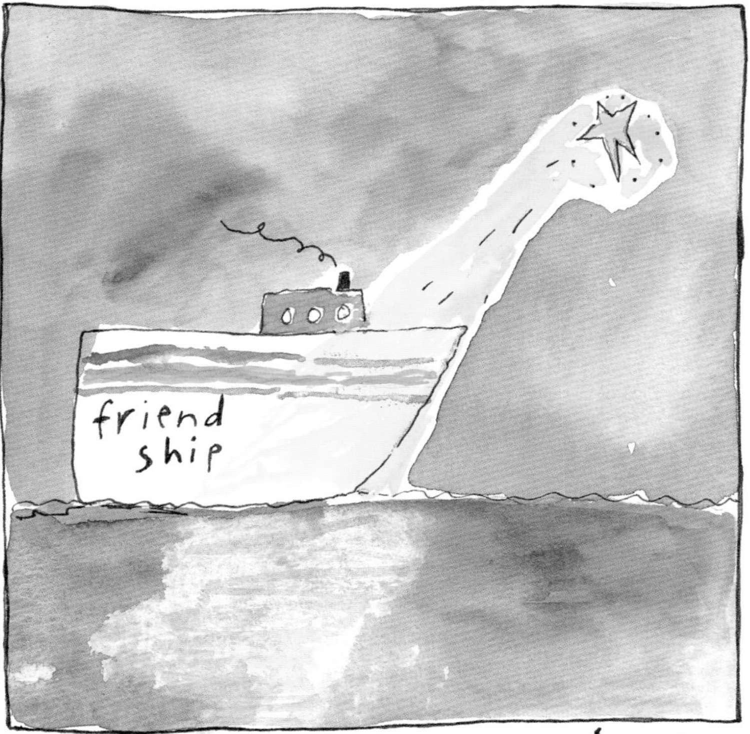

when Life gets dark

Any gesture of heart
(no matter how small)
radiates out

and Touches us all

Like the opposite
of gravity,
friendship
is a force
that lifts us...

and supports us.

When Life unravels...
a friend pushes...
LeT's go
and pats...
There, There..
and helps us shine again.

A friendship is a
baLancing.

It's an up and
downing business.

duck

during mood swings

a friend knows when to dig down deep

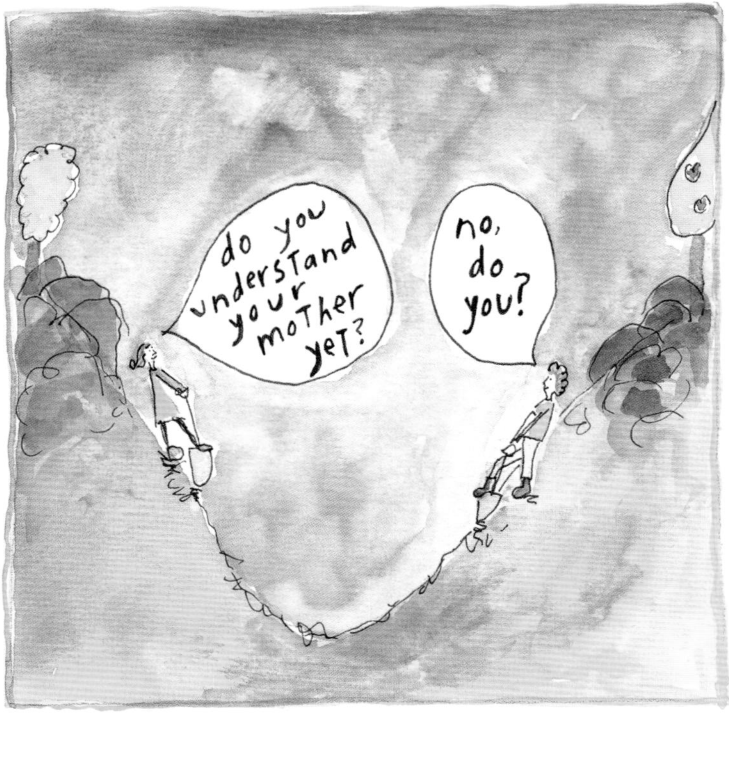

Friendship is what we build

and rebuild...

...even better

THEY KNOW THE VALUE

# of a good drifT

A friend is for
• helping your life
move...
Oh no, noT
anoTher change
van Lines
OLd
STuff
Same

and
just allowing you

heart at rest

To be.

About the Author

Sandy Gingras is an artist and writer with her own design company called "How To Live" (visit her website at www.how-to-live.com). She and her son, three cats and a fat yellow Labrador live next to a salt marsh on Long Beach Island, New Jersey, where she is active in efforts to preserve open space and wetlands.

ⓖ

If you liked this book, you may also enjoy these other books by Sandy Gingras:

The Uh-oh Heart
ISBN 0-945582-96-X
$16.95 hardcover
For all of us with uh-oh hearts fearful of growing and risking and loving.

How To Live on an Island
ISBN 0-945582-57-9
$11.95 hardcover
"...there's no truer place than an island."

Reasons to be Happy at the Beach
ISBN 0-945582-98-6
$16.95 hardcover
"Happiness is...all around us. We are looking at it, breathing it, holding it in our hands."

How To Live at the Beach
ISBN 0-945582-73-0
$12.95 hardcover
"Like the ocean itself, this book nourishes the mind, heart, and soul."
— Coastal Living Magazine

ⓖ

Down The Shore Publishing offers other book and calendar titles (with a special emphasis on the mid-Atlantic coast). For a free catalog, or to be added to our mailing list, just send us a request:

Down The Shore Publishing
P.O. Box 3100
Harvey Cedars, NJ 08008

www.down-the-shore.com

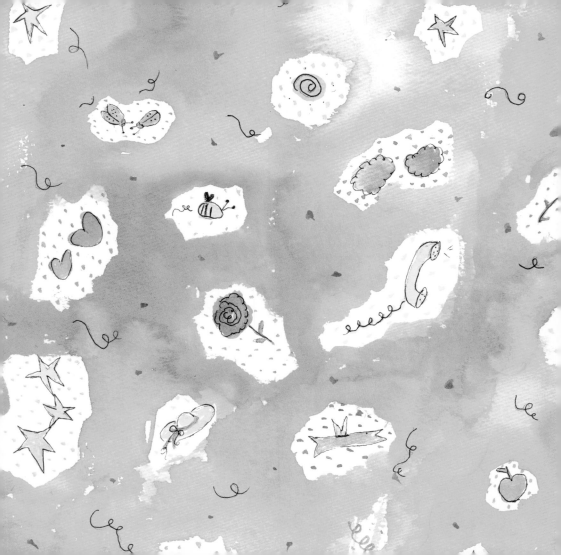